WORLD WAR I AND MODERN AMERICA: 1890–1930

by Lori Fromowitz

Content Consultant
Stephen Stein, PhD
Online Program Director
Department of History, University of Memphis

CORE LIBRARY

Published by ABDO Publishing Company, PO Box 398166, Minneapolis, MN 55439. Copyright © 2014 by Abdo Consulting Group, Inc. International copyrights reserved in all countries. No part of this book may be reproduced in any form without written permission from the publisher. The Core Library™ is a trademark and logo of ABDO Publishing Company.

Printed in the United States of America,
North Mankato, Minnesota
092013
012014
♻ THIS BOOK CONTAINS AT LEAST 10% RECYCLED MATERIALS.

Editor: Jenna Gleisner
Series Designer: Becky Daum

Library of Congress Control Number: 2013945677

Cataloging-in-Publication Data
Fromowitz, Lori.
 World War I and modern America: 1890-1930 / Lori Fromowitz.
   p. cm. -- (The story of the United States)
Includes bibliographical references and index.
ISBN 978-1-62403-177-9
1. United States--History--1865-1921--Juvenile literature. 2. United States--History--1919-1933--Juvenile literature. 3. Progressivism (United States politics)--1865-1933--Juvenile literature. 4. United States--Social life and customs--To 1930--Juvenile literature.   I. Title.
973.91--dc23

                                                      2013945677

Cover: US soldiers board a train and bid farewell to loved ones before leaving for war in 1917.

CONTENTS

THE NEW ERA

In 1891 engineer George Ferris imagined a giant wheel that could carry people high into the air. Many people thought the idea was impossible. The engineer proved everyone wrong. Ferris's wheel was one of the main attractions at the 1893 World's Fair in Chicago, Illinois. The first Ferris wheel rose 264 feet (80 m) in the air. Nearly 26 million people visited the

George Ferris's wheel could carry up to 2,160 people at one time.

1893 World's Fair between May and October. People gathered to see art exhibits and new inventions.

An Industrial Nation

Ferris's wheel was an example of the advances in technology taking place in the United States. This advance in technology was known as the Industrial Revolution. Thomas Edison's new lightbulbs lit up the steel wheel. The United States was becoming an industrial nation. Many people worked in factories in the country's growing cities. Electricity was beginning to change life in the United States. Steam power helped produce goods. It also made traveling by train and boat easier. In 1893 the United States was just beginning a period of change. The country would come to know this time as the beginning of modern America.

The Progressive Era

Many Americans saw that the Industrial Revolution brought problems too. The Industrial Revolution had

Edison's lightbulbs were used to light up Ferris's wheel.

helped some businesses grow very big. These big businesses owned factories, mines, and railroads. Many Americans worried such large businesses held too much power. Businesses could raise prices and force employees to work in terrible conditions. They could even influence the decisions the government made. These and other worries led many citizens to seek reform. Reformers believed average Americans could bring about change. This spirit lasted for the next 30 years. This period of reform, lasting from 1890 to 1920, is known as the Progressive Era.

The 1893 World's Fair was a great success.

Reform for Immigrants

Visitors to the 1893 World's Fair could hear reformer Jane Addams speak. Addams was concerned for US immigrants. During the Progressive Era, the nation experienced a peak of immigration. Most of these immigrants came from Europe. Immigrants often lived and worked in poor, overcrowded conditions. Many Americans, such as Addams, worked to make life better for immigrants.

During the Progressive Era, groups of women fought for suffrage, or the right to vote.

But that same year the United States fell into a financial depression. Many were left poor and jobless. People without jobs marched in protest. People with jobs began to form unions, or groups of workers

Frederick Douglass

Civil rights leader Frederick Douglass spoke at the 1893 World's Fair. Douglass was an admired African-American speaker. At the time African Americans were facing prejudice and violence. Three years earlier, the state of Louisiana had passed a law. This law forced African Americans to ride in separate railway cars from whites. This was the beginning of segregation laws that would become common in the southern states.

who joined together to protect their interests. The depression lasted until 1897.

Progressives worked to bring about changes in many different causes. Some Americans also worried about the pollution industry caused. They wanted to keep the country's green spaces clean. In 1892 John Muir founded the Sierra Club. This club helped protect nature in the Sierra Nevada, a mountain range in Nevada and California.

Prejudice against Africans Americans was another issue facing the country. But some Americans fought prejudice. In 1909 approximately 60 people, including

FURTHER EVIDENCE

Chapter One discusses some of the changes in the United States in the early 1900s, including the Progressive movement. The Web site below also focuses on the Progressive Era. How is the information on the Web site different from the information in this chapter? What information is the same? How do the two sources present information differently? What can you learn from this Web site?

The Progressive Movement
www.mycorelibrary.com/world-war-i-and-modern-america

seven African Americans, formed the National Association for the Advancement of Colored People (NAACP). The group sought justice and equality for African Americans.

CHAPTER TWO

A REACH INTO THE WORLD

While reformers were challenging ideas inside the United States, the nation was also experiencing tension with other countries. In 1895 Cuba had begun to revolt against Spain. Cuba was under Spain's rule, and Cubans felt the Spanish government treated them poorly. The United States had a strong trade relationship with Cuba at the time. Many Americans felt it was important to protect their trade with Cuba.

The Maine sank in Havana Harbor, off the coast of Cuba, in February 1898 after a sudden explosion.

In 1898 the United States sent the battleship *Maine* to protect Americans in Cuba. The *Maine* exploded suddenly near Cuba. Many Americans blamed Spain. They believed Spain had blown up the ship with an underwater mine. The United States responded by demanding that Spain free Cuba. Spain refused. In April 1898, the United States declared war on Spain. To protect and fight, the United States used its strong navy to compete with the most powerful navies in the world.

A Powerful Nation

The United States used its naval power to win the Spanish-American War on July 17, 1898. A peace treaty was signed in December, and Cuba became an independent nation. The United States took control of several of Spain's other territories. During the war, the United States had also taken control of the independent land of Hawaii in the Pacific Ocean. The United States was becoming a powerful nation. It now had a reach into other parts of the world.

A Progressive President

President William McKinley had led the country through the Spanish-American War. He was a popular president. McKinley focused on international issues. He did not bring widespread attention to many of the Progressives' causes. McKinley was shot and killed in September 1901. The new president, Vice President Theodore Roosevelt, was a very different kind of leader.

Roosevelt was an outspoken Progressive. During the Progressive Era, many Americans were concerned with corruption in government. Government leaders sometimes used their power selfishly instead of

Imperialism

The Philippines, Guam, and Puerto Rico were just a few of the Spanish territories the United States claimed after the Spanish-American War. This rule over foreign lands was called imperialism. Many Americans did not approve of it. Some thought it was wrong to rule over people in different countries. They also thought it was not right that the United States had helped Cuba win independence only to take control of other lands.

Conservation President

President Roosevelt worried that westward expansion and industrialization were destroying nature. Roosevelt started the US Forest Service in February 1905. He also set aside certain areas of land as wildlife refuges and created 150 national forests and five national parks. These areas of wilderness were protected from development.

working for the citizens. Roosevelt fought this kind of corruption. He also believed businesses should not have unlimited power. He broke up trusts. These were businesses that grouped together and made it difficult for smaller companies to compete.

Labor Laws

During the Progressive Era, some journalists wrote about problems they saw in US society. They brought these issues to the attention of readers, who were often shocked to learn about them. One problem these journalists wrote about was working conditions. Many laborers worked long hours. They faced unsafe conditions.

One of Roosevelt's biggest concerns was protecting the United States' forests and natural resources.

Accidents from machines were common. Laborers often earned very little money and lived in poverty. These workers were often immigrants, especially in the factories in growing US cities.

Two young girls work in unsafe conditions at a textile, or clothing, mill.

Many poor children worked in factories and mines instead of going to school. The Progressives didn't think children should be treated this way. They demanded better laws to protect children. From 1910 to 1920, the number of child laborers lowered by half. But it would be many years before the government outlawed child labor completely.

Upton Sinclair researched the lives of workers in the meatpacking district of Chicago, Illinois. He wrote about them in his 1906 novel *The Jungle*. In this excerpt, he describes what it was like for one woman working in a meatpacking plant:

> *She was shut up in one of the rooms where the people seldom saw the daylight; beneath her were the chilling rooms, where the meat was frozen, and above her were the cooking rooms; and so she stood on an ice-cold floor, while her head was often so hot that she could scarcely breathe. Trimming beef off the bones by the hundred-weight, while standing up from early morning till late at night, with heavy boots on and the floor always damp and full of puddles.*

Source: Upton Sinclair. "The Jungle." Appeal to Reason May 1905. Print. 2.

Consider Your Audience

Review this passage closely. Consider how you would adapt it for a different audience, such as your parents, your principal, or your friends. Write a blog post conveying this same information for the new audience. How does your blog post differ from the original text and why?

CHAPTER THREE

THE UNITED STATES AND WORLD WAR I

In June 1914, Austria declared war on Serbia. Nations in Europe had made secret agreements to protect one another. Germany promised to support Austria. Russia agreed to help Serbia. Several other European nations soon joined the conflict. Germany and Austria-Hungary were the main nations of what was called the Central Powers. They went to war

Women from the Red Cross bring gifts to US soldiers at a train station before the men leave for war in 1917.

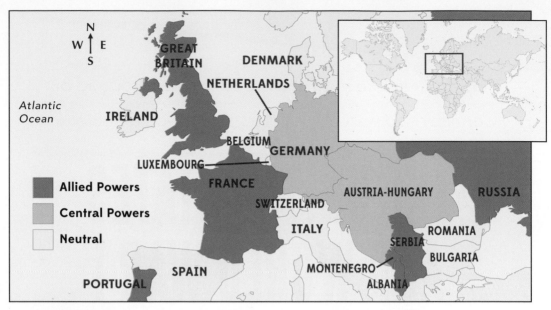

Allied, Central, and Neutral Countries in 1914

Look at the map above. This map shows the Allied, Central, and neutral nations of World War I. How does the map help you understand what it might have been like to move troops to different places in Europe? What do you think it would have been like to live in a neutral nation in Europe during World War I?

against the Allied Powers. Its largest nations were France, Russia, and Great Britain.

The Great War, or World War I (1914–1918), was a bigger war than the world had ever known. Most Americans wanted nothing to do with this conflict overseas. US president Woodrow Wilson also thought the United States should remain neutral, or not take sides.

A Turning Point

This attitude began to change as the war dragged on. Germany had warned travelers that it would sink any ship with an enemy flag, even if it was not a warship. On May 7, 1915, a German U-boat, or submarine, fired a torpedo at the British passenger ship *Lusitania*. The ship sank near Ireland. Nearly 1,200 passengers, including 128 Americans, died.

Americans were angry. They didn't think it was right to attack a ship that was not on a war mission. Many people started to change their opinions about fighting. But it would be still two more years before the United States entered the war.

Declaring War

President Wilson also began to change his mind about going to war. He felt Germany threatened the right of free nations to travel safely and trade freely. He thought countries should not have to worry about more powerful nations invading or controlling them. German attacks on neutral ships continued. In 1917

A New Kind of War

In World War I, a frightening new type of warfare changed the rules of battle. Advances in technology and industrial power brought new weapons. More dangerous guns were used. Tanks were introduced. Eleven years before the war, the US brothers Wilbur and Orville Wright made the first successful airplane flight. World War I was the first major war to make widespread use of airplanes in battle. Battles could now be fought from the air as well as land and sea.

President Wilson asked Congress to declare war on the Central Powers. The United States officially entered World War I on April 6, 1917.

Doughboys at the Front

Between 1917 and 1918, nearly 5 million doughboys, or US soldiers, entered the war in Europe. When they arrived, neither side was winning. Conditions were so bad for the Allied European soldiers that many refused to fight. The Allies had lost many men. The arrival of so many Americans made a difference in the war. It helped raise Allied spirits.

US doughboys fought from camouflaged trenches that hid them from enemy view.

Much of World War I was fought from long ditches called trenches. Soldiers from each side faced each other along nearly 500 miles (805 km) of trench lines. The area in between was called "no-man's-land." The Germans had designed more advanced trenches. Some soldiers had beds and electricity in the trenches. But for the Allied soldiers, life in the

Knit Your Bit!

During World War I, the American Red Cross asked Americans to "knit your bit." Americans at home were asked to knit warm clothes for the soldiers in Europe. One of the things soldiers needed most was warm socks. Soldiers spent long hours standing in trenches filled with water. They had to carry extra pairs of dry socks.

trenches was usually more miserable. They didn't have clean water and lived alongside rats. The battles of World War I were bloody and terrifying for both sides.

The War to End All Wars

As the war went on, the Central Powers suffered from a loss of soldiers. The war ended when Germany surrendered on November 11, 1918. People celebrated the end of World War I. Sixty-five million men from many countries had fought in the war. Nine million men had died. Nearly 21 million soldiers returned home wounded.

President Wilson wanted to create a League of Nations to prevent a future war. This league would

Many soldiers returned home wounded with missing limbs.

guarantee that nations had the right to remain independent and be protected from invasions. As members of the organization, nations would make decisions in the open and enforce these agreements together. Based in Geneva, Switzerland, the League of Nations was formed in 1920. But Congress was concerned about the expenses and difficulties of joining the League of Nations. They decided the United States should not join.

CHAPTER FOUR

A CHANGED NATION

World War I brought big changes for the United States. The country had used its industry and manpower to support the war effort. The nation was now one of the world's biggest economic powers. But by the end of the war, most Americans wanted to stay out of world affairs.

Through the early 1900s, there had been a rise in the number of immigrants coming to the United

Henry Ford experiments with the early stages of his assembly line to build cars in 1913.

States. The war had ended this growth, partly because traveling from Europe was more difficult. At the war's end, many people wanted to leave Europe, which was struggling to rebuild. Many Europeans moved to the United States. People in the United States worried whether their country could handle so many new immigrants. The nation passed new laws about immigration. These laws strictly limited the number of immigrants allowed into the country. The laws also made it difficult for immigrants from certain countries to come to the United States.

The Great Migration

While new immigrants flocked to US shores, some Americans had been on the move since the war began. Slavery had ended in the South after the Civil War (1861–1865). But life was still difficult for African Americans in the South. They continued to face discrimination from segregation laws. Many also were not allowed to vote. Life in the North was not completely free of racism. But for many African

In this 1918 photograph, Henry Ford sits in his first car, which he built in 1896.

Americans, the North offered a chance at a better life. From 1916 to 1970, 6 million Southern African Americans moved to the North. This mass movement was known as the Great Migration.

Many African Americans also hoped for better wages in the North. Most US factories were based in the North. Northern factories that made weapons and other supplies needed workers. Many African Americans in the South moved north in search of factory jobs.

Ford's Big Idea

By the early 1900s, US factories were able to create goods more quickly and cheaply than ever before. Before World War I, factories had started using a new method called an assembly line. Henry Ford had invented the assembly line in an effort to produce automobiles more quickly.

Building Roads and Businesses for Automobiles

By the end of the 1920s, more than half of Americans owned an automobile. These new car owners needed roads to drive on, so the government paved them. Americans were able to travel across the country without taking a train. New businesses such as gas stations and motels were created to serve these new drivers.

Ford thought the automobile was a fine machine. But the first automobiles were handcrafted. Only the rich could afford them. Ford wanted to make an automobile that working Americans could buy. He realized he would have to build automobiles more quickly and cheaply to do this.

US Motor Vehicle Registration Rates 1895–1929			
Year	Cars	Trucks	Total Vehicles
1895	4	-	4
1900	8,000	-	8,000
1905	77,400	600	78,000
1910	458,500	10,000	468,500
1915	2,309,666	136,000	2,445,666
1920	8,225,859	1,006,082	9,231,941
1925	17,512,638	2,441,709	19,954,347
1929	23,121,589	3,379,854	26,501,443

Rise of Automobiles

The chart above shows the number of automobiles registered with the government in the United States from 1895 to 1929. How did US vehicle ownership change over time? In which years do you see the biggest increase in car ownership? How might life be different today if Ford's idea had not been successful?

In December 1913 the workers at Ford's auto plant began using an assembly line to build automobiles. A belt rolled out the product. Each worker did an assigned task on the product as the belt moved the product along. This type of

Prohibition

Among the many changes taking place in the United States at the beginning of the 1900s was the victory of the temperance movement. Temperance supporters viewed alcohol as a terrible problem for the nation. Beginning in January 1920, the Eighteenth Amendment was enforced. This amendment enacted Prohibition, which made it illegal for Americans to buy and sell alcohol. Despite the law, many people still bought and sold alcohol illegally. Prohibition remained the law until 1933.

production made goods more affordable. Ford's plan to build and sell an affordable car was successful. The assembly line helped turn the United States into a nation of automobiles, drivers, and roads. In the years following the war, more Americans bought cars. Soon assembly lines were rolling out more than cars.

Nineteenth Amendment

The assembly line improved the US economy. The nation was also changing in other ways. Women had been fighting for suffrage since the 1800s. During World War I, as many men fought overseas, nearly 1 million women had joined the workforce. Many worked in factories and made supplies for the war. Thousands of women served in the US Army and US Navy Nursing Corps overseas. Many felt it was not fair to expect women to help in wartime if they could not vote. This opinion helped women gain suffrage. On August 24, 1920, Congress ratified the Nineteenth Amendment. This amendment gave women the right to vote.

EXPLORE ONLINE

Chapter Four discusses the Nineteenth Amendment and women's right to vote. The Web site below also focuses on the suffrage struggle and the effects of the Nineteenth Amendment. As you know, every source is different. How is the information on the Web site different from the information in this chapter? What information is the same? How do the two sources present information differently? What can you learn from this Web site?

Women Struggle for an Equal Voice

www.mycorelibrary.com/world-war-i-and-modern-america

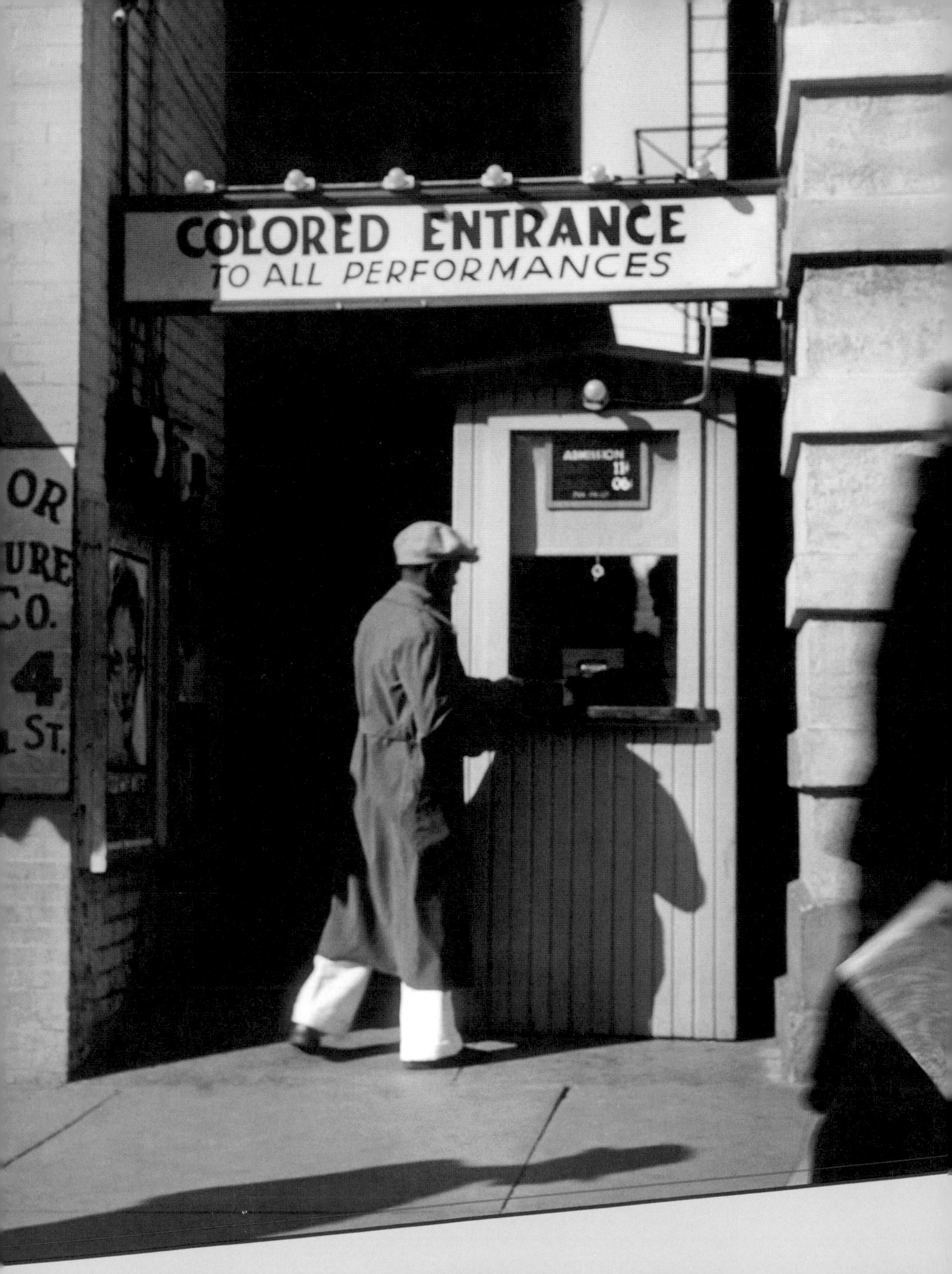
COLORED ENTRANCE
TO ALL PERFORMANCES

CHAPTER FIVE

THE ROARING TWENTIES

After World War I, African Americans continued to seek justice and equality. In the 1920s they also sought economic and business success. This movement became known as the Harlem Renaissance. It lasted until the mid-1930s. The movement encouraged pride among African Americans in their heritage.

An African-American man buys a theater ticket from a segregated booth.

The Harlem Renaissance

The cultural center of this movement was in the Harlem neighborhood in New York City. There, thinkers, artists, and musicians formed one of the most exciting artistic and cultural periods in US history. Writers such as Langston Hughes and Zora Neale Hurston were important voices of the time. They and many others wrote about their experiences as African Americans. Their works influenced people around the country.

Langston Hughes

Langston Hughes first came to New York to attend Columbia University. Within a short time, he was an important voice of the Harlem Renaissance. Hughes experimented with new ways to write poetry. He wanted to represent the African-American people. Hughes first became known during the Harlem Renaissance, but he had a long career as a writer.

Boom Times

The exciting pace and booming economy of the 1920s contributed to another nickname for the time period: the Roaring Twenties. The use of the assembly line, the

Langston Hughes wrote novels, plays, and poems that inspired African-American pride during and after the Harlem Renaissance.

growth of economy, and the spread of electricity and roads completed the modernization that had begun at the end of the Industrial Era. More Americans left rural areas for cities. As cars became a part of life for Americans, suburbs began to grow around cities. At the same time, passengers were able to travel on the first commercial airline flights. Some people were becoming very wealthy by investing money in the stock market.

The Jazz Age

At night, Harlem's nightclubs were packed with audiences who came to hear jazz music. Developed by African-American musicians, jazz featured uneven rhythms. Jazz became popular with white audiences as well. It became an influential art form. This music was so popular in the 1920s that it gave the era another one of its nicknames: The Jazz Age.

The New America

On Tuesday, October 29, 1929, the roar of the 1920s came to a stop. The stock market crashed, beginning the Great Depression. In the last 40 years, the United States had become a modern country. The land was crisscrossed with highways. Women could vote, and reformers had made their voices heard. The United States was now an important world power. The nation was about to face some of its biggest challenges, but it was ready for what the future might hold.

"Mother to Son" is one of Langston Hughes's earliest poems. In it he writes in the voice of a woman speaking to her son:

> Well, son, I'll tell you:
> Life for me ain't been no crystal stair.
>
> . . .
>
> But all the time
> I'se been a-climbin' on,
>
> . . .
>
> And sometimes goin' in the dark
> Where there ain't been no light.
> So, boy, don't you turn back.
>
> . . .
>
> Source: Langston Hughes. "Mother to Son." The Crisis December 1922. Print. 87.

What's the Big Idea?

Read the poem closely. What might one of the poem's main ideas be? How does using the voice of a mother speaking to a son contribute to this main idea? How do the experiences discussed in this poem relate to the topics in this chapter?

IMPORTANT DATES

1892

John Muir founds the Sierra Club to appreciate and protect nature.

1893

Nearly 26 million people attend the World's Fair in Chicago, Illinois.

1898

The Spanish-American War begins in April. The United States wins the war, proving it has a powerful navy.

1913

Henry Ford's assembly line starts rolling in December, helping make cars and other goods more affordable.

1917

The United States enters World War I on April 6. Europe has been involved in the war since 1914.

1918

World War I ends on November 11 after Germany surrenders.

1901

President William McKinley is assassinated in September. Vice President Theodore Roosevelt becomes president.

1906

Upton Sinclair's novel *The Jungle* is published, sharing details of the meatpacking industry in Chicago.

1909

A group of reformers form the National Association for the Advancement of Colored People to protect civil rights and advance racial equality.

1920

Prohibition begins in the United States in January. Buying and selling alcohol becomes illegal until 1933.

1920

Women gain the right to vote when the Nineteenth Amendment is ratified on August 24.

1929

The stock market crashes on October 29, signaling the beginning of the Great Depression.

Surprise Me

Chapters Four and Five discuss some of the changes that occurred in the United States following World War I. After reading this book, what are two or three facts about the changes that you found surprising? Write a sentence about each fact. Why did you find them surprising?

Take a Stand

This book discusses why the United States entered World War I. Do you think the country should have gone to war or chosen to remain neutral? Why or why not? Write a short essay explaining your opinion. Make sure to give reasons for your opinion and facts and details to support those reasons.

You Are There

Chapters One and Two of this book discuss the lives of immigrants in the United States at the turn of the century. Imagine you are an immigrant working in a factory. What is your life like? What do you think about the other workers or the factory owners? Write a short description of your typical day in the factory.

Say What?

Studying US history can mean learning a lot of new vocabulary. Find five words in this book you have never seen or heard before. Use a dictionary to find out what they mean. Then write the meanings in your own words. Use each word in a new sentence.

GLOSSARY

conservation
the act of avoiding waste and saving resources

economy
the state or management of the money and resources of a nation, state, city, or territory

engineer
a designer of engines, machines, or bridges

immigrant
a person who moves from one country to another to live

neutral
not involved with either side

progressive
seeking change or advancement

ratified
approved

segregation
the act of keeping different groups apart

suffrage
the right to vote

temperance
the act of limiting or avoiding consumption of alcohol

trench
a ditch or groove in the ground

union
a group of workers that join together to bargain for pay and better work conditions

LEARN MORE

Books

Goldsworthy, Steve. *World War I*. New York: Weigl, 2013.

Jeffrey, Gary. *War in the Air*. Ontario: Crabtree, 2013.

Oxlade, Chris. *World War I*. Mankato, MN: Arcturus, 2011.

Web Links

To learn more about the United States and World War I, visit ABDO Publishing Company online at **www.abdopublishing.com**. Web sites about the United States and World War I are featured on our Book Links page. These links are routinely monitored and updated to provide the most current information available.

Visit **www.mycorelibrary.com** for free additional tools for teachers and students.

INDEX

ABOUT THE AUTHOR

Lori Fromowitz is a writer and editor of children's educational material. She graduated from Bard College, where she studied theater and playwriting. Lori is currently attending graduate school. She lives in Somerville, Massachusetts.